# THE BEST OF
# PRAGUE

## PHOTOGRAPHIC GUIDE

**The Best of Prague**
© **AGENTURA ROKA**
ROKA'S GUIDES 1996, 1998, 2000
english version
third edition, Prague 2000

**conception** Vladimír Purgert
**editor** Roman Kapr
**versions** czech, dutch, english, french,
german, italien, russian, spanish

**text** Roman Kapr
**photo** Roman Maleček, Jan Reich,
Bohumil Landisch, Dalibor Kusák, Antonín Srch,
Libor Hajský, Roman Kapr, Vladimír Purgert
**translation** Překladatelský servis Skřivánek Ltd.
**map** SHO-Cart Ltd.
**scheme** ROKA

**graphic arrangement** Roman Kapr
**composition** ROKA
**scanning** Leonardo Ltd.
**lithography, print and hard-cover**
POINT CZ Ltd.

**number of pages** 120
**number of pictures** 175

**special thanks due to** Prague Tourist Centers

**distributed by**
ROKA CENTRE Ltd., Na Jezerce 14, CZ - Prague 4,
Tel. 00-420-608-202050
URL: http://www.roka.cz
e-mail: centre@roka.cz

ISBN 80-902000-0-1

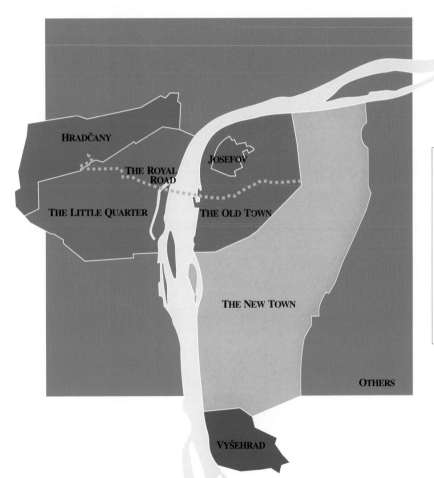

HRADČANY

JOSEFOV

THE ROYAL ROAD

THE LITTLE QUARTER

THE OLD TOWN

THE NEW TOWN

OTHERS

VYŠEHRAD

**CONTENTS**      **page**

SCHEME     3
PREFACE     5

**THE ROYAL ROAD**     **6**
**HRADČANY**     **26**
**THE LITTLE QUARTER**     **48**
**JOSEFOV**     **64**
**THE OLD TOWN**     **74**
**THE NEW TOWN**     **96**
**VYŠEHRAD**     **106**
**OTHERS**     **112**

MAP     120

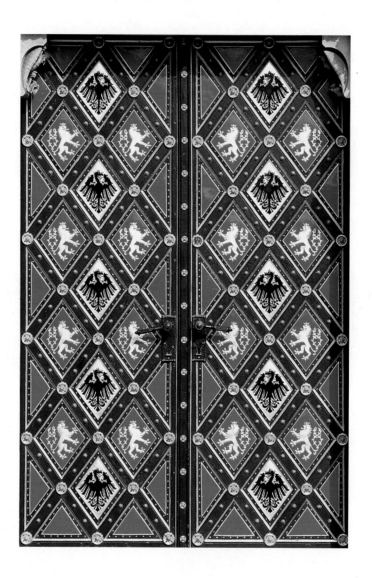

**For several centuries, it has been possible to claim that no other inland European city offers so many wonderful sights** as Prague does. That's why even in the distant past, Aeneas Sylvius called it the "Pearl of All Cities", and Goethe said about Prague that in the crown of the cities, Prague is the most precious stone. Alex. Humboldt puts Prague - as concerns its beauty - on the fourth place among European cities and on the first place as concerns the inland cities. Viollet-le-Duc, a French architect and an outstanding connoisseur of European architecture enthusiastically said that Prague is a beautiful city which is marvelously built, has a hitherto prevailingly mediaeval nature and is crowned with an acropolis that makes an impression of a magnificent Gothic castle, and he also added that historical monuments of Prague are marked by their rich contents and a remarkable aristocratic character which, however, is not at the expense of picturesqueness. Also, for example William Ritter, a French critic and esthetician, writes about Prague that nowhere on this Earth, there is an open book of history and architecture that would be more splendid.

We tried to concentrate much of this unique Prague architecture, the architecture of one millennium, in our photographic guide. And there are several historic relations which give the idea why the architecture has been preserved so fully in this very place and what were the moving forces in this region. Let us take a deeper look at them, I think that they do not lack a dramatic form both in the revolutionary times and in the seemingly rigid times because for Europe, Bohemia is the battlefield between its Eastern and Central part. It is a very favourable location, sometimes an excellent one which does not lack sufficient natural resources. The natural conditions favoured the East, facilitating access from this direction and inhibiting the access from the West. This perhaps explains the fact that of the three great nations, Celts, Germans and Slavs which took turns in residing in Bohemia, the the most Eastern of them gained dominance, and that those who eventually stayed did not share the fate of the Slavs to the North or to the South of them. This is why the Czechs are located most westward of all Slavs, and with their cultural life and their ability to defend themselves, they were to prove the justifiability of their position on the dividing line of West and East Europe. The original colonization started from the rivers and along rivers and the settlements were also different in the hilly regions from the ones in the lowland central region. Concentrated, round villages originating in one single family yard, are the Slavic settlements. Individual buildings scattered around the countryside, sometimes in a long row, are the German settlements. It was Germans, mostly on the periphery of Bohemia, who displayed the ability to colonize and farm the hilly regions. In places where the need for protection did not cram the population into towns surrounded by ramparts, up until now it is distinguishable which of the two nationalities colonized and cleared the original forest. It was this blending of these two nations which created that cultural atmosphere in Bohemia which Prague grew in, and all this was "seasoned" with the works of Italians, Spaniards, Frenchmen, Austrians who were invited by the ruling dynasties. The many-year co-existence with an "empire which ruled Danube" can also be explained by the easy accessability of Bohemia from this direction, from the southeast. Numerous ruins remind that even in the history of Bohemia, times of peaceful development are followed by pernicious wars which, however, since the thirty-year war and apart from the last century had no marked impact on the cultural development and thus on the building activity and architecture. This is documented, above all, by the historical centre of the city of Prague which remained undamaged as if by a miracle. Let us summarize it all by quoting what's under the headword Bohemia in Otto's Educative Dictionary published in the year 1893: "The comparative history tells us that even national dualism which, as any other one, is an incentive to a persistent advancement according to the laws of Nature, which advancement results from the application of all powers in the thousand-year-old struggle. If Bohemia stands higher than the other countries in respect to education and wealth, it can thank for it to the ancient struggle both of the two seas and of the two great nations whose waves crash against each other in Bohemia".

The guide is divided into eight parts: Royal Road, Hradčany, Little Quarter, Josefov, Old Town, New Town, Vyšehrad and Others. All of these, with the exception of the Royal Road and Others, are historical Prague towns. The parts are distinguished by colour and the historical monuments photographed that are shown in each part are in places which, when linked within the frame of such part, form an itinerary that can be followed. This effect is supported by the exact address shown at the very bottom below each picture. Above the picture, there is the description of the historical monument or possibly some related curiosity where the text is in boldface. So, there is nothing more to say but to wish you much pleasant experience.

Roman Kapr

# THE ROYAL ROAD

The Royal Road (Královská cesta), also called the Coronation Road, which ends in Prague Castle (Pražský hrad) at St. Vit's Cathedral (chrám sv. Víta), used to start in the Old Town of Prague at Powder Gate (Prašná brána) which was founded in the year 1475. Through this gate, the coronation processions of Czech kings used to start along the Celetná street, one of the oldest streets of Prague which was a part of an important route from East Bohemia, especially from the town of Kutná Hora, as early as in the period of Romanesque style, to the main Prague market on the present Old Town Square (Staroměstské náměstí) which was called the Great Square at that time. The Royal Road then continues across Small Square (Malé náměstí), along Charles' street (Karlova) and Charles' Bridge (Karlův most), the jewel of European Gothic architecture and Baroque sculpture, Mostecká street, across Malostranské Square, the centre of Little Quarter (Malá Strana) with St. Nicholas' Church (kostel sv. Mikuláše), along Nerudova street and across Hradčanské Square to the aforementioned Prague Castle and St. Vit's Cathedral situated on the castle yard III.

Today, this Road is a masterly combination of Gothic, Renaissance, Baroque, Classicism, Art Nouveau and Cubism and, in a figurative meaning, it is entitled to be called the Royal Road because with its route, it not only intersects but, above all, imaginarily connects the cultural riches of Prague.

**house At Golden Angel**
*[Praha 1, Staré Město, Celetná 29]*

**house At Black Sun**
*[Praha 1, Staré Město, Celetná 8]*

**monument of Roman Emperor Charles IV.**
*[Praha 1, Staré Město, Křižovnické náměstí]*

**sculpture of St. Jan Nepomucký, detail**
*[Praha 1, Karlův most]*

**house At Three Violins**
*[Praha 1, Malá Strana, Nerudova 12]*

**sculptural group of Struggling Giants**
*[Praha 1, Hradčany, yard I. of Prague Castle]*

the present appearance of **Powder Tower** comes from the years 1875-86 (pseudo-Gothic style). The tower is called „Powder" since the end of the 17th century when it served as the storehouse of gunpowder

*[Praha 1, Staré Město, view from the building of the Czech National Bank - Na příkopě 28]*

**Celená Street** whose name is derived from the word „calty" designating plaited buns made by local bakers here
*[Praha 1, Staré Město, seen from Hrzán Palace from Harasov - Celetná 12]*

**Old Town Square** at the end of Celetná Street with (from the left) house At White Unicorn, Sixt's house, house At Stone Virgin Mary, house At Stone Lamb, house At Stone Table
*[Praha 1, Staré Město, Staroměstské náměstí 15, Celetná 2, Staroměstské náměstí 16, 17, 18]*

unique **Old Town Astronomical Clock** created as early as at the beginning of the 15th century by Mikuláš from the town of Kadaň, a clockmaker
*[Praha 1, Staré Město, Staroměstské náměstí 3]*

**Old Town Hall** where, at the time when they had been at the zenith of their power, the Czech local governors elected Jiří from Poděbrady as the Czech king in the year 1458
*[Praha 1, Staré Město, Staroměstské náměstí 3]*

early-Baroque front of **house At Golden Well** with plaster reliefs of plague patron saints
*[Praha 1, Staré Město, Karlova 3]*

detail of the 1st floor of **Old Town Bridge Tower** next to which there are statues of St. Vít, the patron saint of Charles Bridge, and the sitting figures of Charles IV. and Wenceslas IV.
*[Praha 1, Staré Město, Křižovnické náměstí]*

east part of **Charles Bridge** with early-Baroque building of the former seat of supreme representatives of church and with Old Town Bridge Tower standing on the first pier of the bridge
*[Praha 1, Staré Město, Karlův most resp. Křižovnické náměstí]*

detail of the **group of sculptures of Madonna with St. Bernard** by M.V. Jäckel from the year 1709
*[Praha 1, Karlův most]*

half of the same group of sculptures that were created at the expense of abbot of Osek, Ben. Littwerig

**sculpture of St. Augustin** by J.B. Kohl from the year 1708
*[Praha 1, Karlův most]*

**Charles Bridge** at sunrise with the skyline of Old Town
*[Praha 1, Karlův most]*

**Charles Bridge** was founded in the year 1357 approximately in the place where the former Romanesque Juditha's bridge (built around the year 1170) had been which was damaged by a flood in the year 1342. The construction of Charles Bridge which is 520 m long and 10 m wide, with sixteen arches, was managed by Petr Parléř. The exact date of its completion is not known and it is presumed that the completion took place sometime around the beginning of the 15th century. Originally, the bridge had been called Prague Bridge or Stone Bridge until the year 1870 when the bridge was renamed to Charles Bridge in honour of the founder of the bridge, Roman Emperor and Czech king Charles IV. There are thirty statues and groups of sculptures of saints on each side of the bridge which were being installed there one by one from the year 1683. The bridge as well as the sculptures (except for two of them) are hewn out of Czech sandstones

*[Praha 1, Karlův most as seen from Kampa]*

a marvelous view of **Charles Bridge** and **Prague Castle** any time of the day from the gallery of Old Town Bridge Tower open to the public
*[Praha 1, Karlův most, Malá Strana resp. Hradčany]*

morning sun above **Charles Bridge** in late autumn
[Praha 1, Karlův most]

Gothic **Bridge Towers of The Little Quarter** with St. Nicholas' Church, the most notable construction of Prague Baroque, in the background
*[Praha 1, Staré Město, Karlův most resp. Malostranské náměstí]*

**house At Two Suns** with dominant early-Baroque gables from the year 1673 where Jan Neruda, a poet whose name this street bears, lived from the year 1845
*[Praha 1, Malá Strana, Nerudova 47]*

**castle yard I. of Prague Castle** surrounded by buildings built in the years 1759 - 69 in the style of Italian-Vienna Classicism with Matthias' Gate in the middle
*[Praha 1, Hradčany, Pražský hrad]*

# HRADČANY

Hradčany were, as the third town of Prague, founded at the beginning of the 14th century by a Royal Count Berka from Dubé. At that time, however, there was already the Prague Castle, formerly called Royal Castle, a historical-political and cultural dominating feature of not only Hradčany and Prague, but of the whole Bohemia, influencing with its significance the whole Central Europe for centuries, whose foundation dates back sometime after 880 A.D. Soon after its foundation, Czech princes moved their residence here from Levý Hradec. This choice was of great importance both to the fate of the castle and to the fate of the future city. The reign of Charles IV. and the later reign of Rudolph II., when the Castle was the residence of a Roman Emperor, were important periods in the history of the Castle and therefore, at the time of reconstructions, the Castle's residential importance was expressed. Another marked constructional period was the 2nd half of the 18th century when the Habsburgs had the Castle extensively reconstructed according to the plans of Nicola Pacassi from Vienna, an architect. The jewels of the Castle's architecture are the Gothic St. Vit's Cathedral where the coronation jewels are deposited and the tomb of Czech rulers is found, the Old Royal Palace (Starý královský palác) with Vladislav's Hall (Vladislavský sál), Romanesque church and the former St. George's Monastery (kostel sv. Jiří), Spanish Hall (Španělský sál) in the wing of the castle yard II and other places such as Golden Street (Zlatá ulička). Outside the premises of the Castle, other places of interest are the Royal Garden (Královská zahrada) with the Royal Summerhouse (Královský letohrádek), Loretánské Square with Loreta, Angel Virgin Mary's Church (kostel P. Marie Andělské) and Černín Palace, and last but not the least, the Strahov Monastery (Strahovský klášter) with a unique library.

Since the year 1918, Prague Castle has been the residence of the president of Czechoslovak Republic, or of Czech Republic as it is today.

**castle guard**
[Praha 1, Hradčany, yard I. of Prague Castle]

**house sign of the Baroque palace of Hložek's**
[Praha 1, Hradčany, Kanovnická 4]

**Organ-grinder**
[Praha 1, Hradčany, Hradčanské náměstí]

**south face of Archbishop Palace**
[Praha 1, Hradčany, Hradčanské náměstí 16]

**cast bronze relief above the gates of St. Vít's Cathedral**
[Praha 1, Hradčany, yard III. of Prague Castle]

**detail of the body tube of the Singing Fountain**
[Praha 1, Hradčany, Královská zahrada]

**St. Vít's Cathedral** and the **south face of the Old Palace** of Prague Castle from the garden called Na valech which is also accessible via the decorative stairs from the castle yard III.
*[Praha 1, Hradčany, zahrada Na valech]*

a few steps from the 1st castle courtyard stands a remarkable, late Baroque **Archbishop's Palace**, the seat of Prague's archbishopric from 1562
*[Praha 1, Hradčany, Hradčanské náměstí 16]*

romantic evening in the **street Nový Svět** (New World), suburb of Hradčany, formerly the district of less wealthy population which, however, is very picturesque with unassuming Baroque houses today

*[Praha 1, Hradčany, Nový Svět 19]*

**Loreta**, a place of pilgrimage called after the copy of Loreta Chapel. In the tower, there is a famous Marian glockenspiel made by P. Naumann, a clockmaker, in the year 1694
*[Praha 1, Hradčany, Loretánské náměstí 7]*

panorama of Hradčany and the Old Town with a reflection of Vltava. In the front, there is a very important **Strahov Monastery** of Premonstratensians founded as early as in the year 1140
*[Praha 1, Hradčany, Strahovské nádvoří 1]*

**Philosophical Hall** of the monastery with a collection of Baroque book bindings and a ceiling painting The History of Mankind by A. F. Maulbertsch, the most prominent painter of Vienna Rococo
*[Praha 1, Hradčany, Strahovský klášter]*

north-west view of Saint Vitus Cathedral from the **Summer Riding-School**, built in addition to the extensive Winter Riding-School. The orchard terrace in between the riding-schools is the work of O. Rothmayer

*[Praha 1, Hradčany, ul. U Prašného mostu]*

a jewel of European Gothic, **St. Vít's Cathedral** where the coronation jewels of the Bohemian Kingdom are deposited and where the bodies of the Czech rulers are buried
*[Praha 1, Hradčany, yard III. of Prague Castle]*

**Spanish hall**, built in the years 1602 to 1606 in the reign of the emperor Rudolph II., a member of Habsburg dynasty
*[Praha 1, Hradčany, north wing of castle yard II.]*

slim Gothic style of the nave of **St. Vít's Cathedral**
*[Praha 1, Hradčany, yard III. of Prague Castle]*

**Vladislav's Hall**, the largest secular indoor space of mediaeval Prague which is 62 m long, 16 m wide and 13 m high and which is the most splendid hall of the Central European late Gothic in general too. At present, particularly the election of the president of Czech Republic take place here. It has been used for large celebrations since the 1st half of the 16th century when tournaments of knights also took place here, it was an assembly point at times of assemblies and there were also selling counters of courtly merchants
*[Praha 1, Hradčany, Old Royal Palace of Prague Castle]*

**Old Chamber**, the place of sessions of the supreme land court and assemblies of the representatives of Czech local governors until the year 1847
*[Praha 1, Hradčany, Old Royal Palace of Prague Castle]*

late Gothic ribbed vault of **equestrian stairs** which made it possible to enter the Vladislav's Hall even on horses
*[Praha 1, Hradčany, Old Royal Palace of Prague Castle]*

the front of **St. George's Church**, the best preserved Romanesque hist. monument in Prague which was put into present appearance at the time of Mother Superior Berta after the fire of the Castle in the year 1142

*[Praha 1, Hradčany, náměstí U sv. Jiří]*

a popular place in the Castle, the **Golden Street** with colourfully painted one-storey houses. The street is called after the goldbeaters of Rudolph II. who had lived here, just as Franz Kafka did in later times

*[Praha 1, Hradčany, Zlatá ulička]*

autumn picture of **Chotkovy Orchards** founded in the year 1832
*[Praha 1, Hradčany, Chotkovy sady]*

again, **Chotkovy Orchards**. Behind the trees, the Royal Summerhouse can be seen
*[Praha 1, Hradčany, Chotkovy sady]*

giardinetto with the Singing Fountain and the **Royal Summerhouse**, a piece of the purest Renaissance architecture outside Italian land, finished in the year 1563
*[Praha 1, Hradčany, Královská zahrada]*

the **Singing Fountain** standing in front of it comes from the same period. Its name is derived from the sound of the drops of water which fall from the upper on the lower bowl of the fountain
*[Praha 1, Hradčany, Královská zahrada]*

# THE LITTLE QUARTER

The Little Quarter (Malá Strana), originally called the New Town of Prague and later on called The Minor Town of Prague, was founded by the king Přemysl Otakar II. in the year 1257. However, as early as in the 8th century, there was a market settlement here. After the foundation of the Town, the original settlers were replaced by colonists of mostly foreign nationalities. Charles IV. extended the Minor Town of Prague by other plots of land but the Town remained, thanks to several great fires apart from other things, more backward in respect to economy than, and politically dependent on, the Towns on the right bank of Vltava. From the 16th century, feudalists and church orders which gave this part of the city its present appearance, and not only architectural one, gradually started to settle here. As a consequence of this, this part of the city includes Wallenstein Palace (Valdštejnský palác) with its garden, St. Nicholas' Cathedral, Thun, Buquoy, Fürstenberg, Hartig, Kaiserstein, Kolowrat, Lichtenstein, Schönborn, Lobkowicz Palaces and many other ones; there are often more palaces per one dynasty. This is also one of the reasons why this part of the city became the residence of many embassies, but also of Czech Parliament and the government which resides in the buildings of the former "Straka's Academy".

It seems that Little Quarter has been pervaded with a sort of mysterious spirit from the 15th century up until now, resulting perhaps from the spoiled chance to become the main district of Prague, perhaps from the confined space between the two hills and a river, but it can also be the spirit of diplomacy which has been and is practiced perhaps in every third house. Whatever it is, it gives this part of the city an original and, towards future, fully conscious character.

**view from the Lookout tower on the hill Petřín**
*[Praha 1, Malá Strana, Petřín]*

**Lookout tower on the hill Petřín, built in the year 1891**
*[Praha 1, Malá Strana, Petřínská rozhledna]*

**house At Blue Fox**
*[Praha 1, Malá Strana, Na Kampě 1]*

**plague column from the year 1715**
*[Praha 1, Malá Strana, Malostranské náměstí]*

**sign of the house At Golden Glass**
*[Praha 1, Malá Strana, Nerudova 16]*

**copy of the sculpture by Antonín Braun**
*[Praha 1, Malá Strana, Klárov]*

view from **Chateau Stairs** constructed in the year 1674 on the mediaeval walls of the fortification of Prague Castle. Niches on the left were originally intended for shops, later on for sculptures

*[Praha 1, Malá Strana, Nové zámecké schody]*

the **Sternberg Palace**, now used by the CR Parliament, experienced in 1541 probably the most damaging fire Prague had ever seen. The palace's present appearance dates back to the end of the 17th century
*[Praha 1, Malá Strana, Malostranské náměstí 19]*

the garden of the **Wallenstein Palace** in front with the monumental sala terrena from 1627, which for example staged the Schiller's Wallenstein in 1853. In front of the sala terrena, there is a giardinetto with a bronze fountain from the year 1630 and a casting of the original sculpture of Venus with amoretto by B. Wurzelbauer from the year 1599. In the foreground, there are castings of the original bronze sculptures of antique deities and horses created by Adriaen de Vries, a sculptor, in the years 1626 to 1627. The originals of these sculptures have been in Drootningholm Chateau in Sweden from the year 1648 where they were transported by Swedes as a loot gained in war. The towers of St. Vít's Cathedral rise above sala terrena

[Praha 1, Malá Strana, Valdštejnské náměstí 4]

the main hall of Wallenstein Palace in its front wing. This hall is called **Knight Hall** and is decorated with a plaster vault with the figures of geniuses, military emblems and a ceiling painting repr. Albrecht as Mars

*[Praha 1, Malá Strana, Valdštejnské náměstí 4]*

bottom right, on the corner of the Malostr. square, stands hist. the most sig. building in the Little Quarter, a former city hall, now called **Malostranská beseda**. A view from the tower at the Church of St. Nicolas

*[Praha 1, Malá Strana, Malostranské náměstí 21]*

the area of the nave of **St. Nicholas' Church** with the system of intersecting ellipsoids is the most magnificent example of the pompousness of Baroque at its zenith in Prague
*[Praha 1, Malá Strana, Malostranské náměstí]*

the front of **St. Nicholas' Church** which was finished in the style called „illusive Baroque of Roman school" in the year 1710. The church forms the south side of former Jesuit college

*[Praha 1, Malá Strana, Malostranské náměstí]*

**Vojan's Orchards**, formerly the garden of the monastery of Barefoot Carmelites, which came into being around the year 1670 and where the monastic origin is documented by two chapels
*[Praha 1, Malá Strana, U lužického semináře 17]*

bridge over **Čertovka**, a branch of Vltava, dividing the island Kampa from the Little Quarter
*[Praha 1, Malá Strana, Kampa]*

**Velkopřevorský Mill** which stood here since the year 1400 is the only intact representative of the old Prague mills
*[Praha 1, Malá Strana, Velkopřevorské náměstí 6]*

the front of the **monastery of Maltese Knights Order**, Johanites, founded in the year 1158 by chancellor Gervasius with the support of king Vladislav I. as the first Czech institution of this order
*[Praha 1, Malá Strana, Velkopřevorské náměstí 4]*

vases and sculptures of Antique gods - craftsmanship mastery by M. Braun in a beautiful Baroque terraced **Vrtbovská garden**, now reconstructed, with a sight-seeing terrace and a lovely view of Prague
*[Praha 1, Malá Strana, Vrtbovská zahrada]*

**Valley of the Little Quarter** below Prague Castle as seen from Strahov Garden in autumn
*[Praha 1, Malá Strana, taken from Strahovská zahrada]*

in the foreground, the dome and part of the front of **St. Nicholas' Church** as seen from the terrace in front of Prague Castle in the evening
*[Praha 1, Malá Strana, Malostranské náměstí]*

# JOSEFOV

Josefov, formerly Jewish Town, came into being from a settlement of Jewish traders and moneychangers that was adjacent to the ancient ford over Vltava on the north tip of the "Slavic Flood Island" which extended from a place presently opposite to the National Theater (Národní divadlo) as far as Kaprova Street in the original riverbed of Vltava. Due to mediaeval antisemitism, the Town had firm ramparts with gates whose number totalled to seven in the year 1848. The Town was also self-governed with the Jews being direct serfs of the ruler. Life in this Town was very hard for most of the Jews for the reason of the impossibility to extend built-up area and of several deportations from Bohemia alone. This persisted until Joseph II. whose name the Jewish Town bears today granted the Town equal rights in his religious reforms in the second half of the 18th century. At the beginning of the 20th century, the old buildings were redeveloped and thus Josefov fully merged with the surrounding Old Town. However, such remarkable historical monuments as the Old Jewish Cemetery (Starý židovský hřbitov) and Old-New (Staronová), Pinkas', Maisel's, Klausová or Spanish (Španělská) synagogues were preserved.

The Jewish Town gives Prague yet another dimension which includes such names as Marek Mordechal Mayzl, a primate, Jakub Bassevi, a trader, Jehuda Löw Ben Bezalel - the famous rabbi Löw or Franz Kafka, a writer. This dimension undisputedly enhances Prague's cultural fullness, whether in respect to trade, science, art or lifestyle.

**house sign on Jewish Town Hall**
[Praha 1, Josefov, Maiselova 18]

**front of Maisel's Synagogue**
[Praha 1, Josefov, Maiselova 10]

**porcelain sculpture of a woman with carps**
[Praha 1, Josefov, Žatecká 8]

**Hebrew table on Staronová Synagogue**
[Praha 1, Josefov, Červená 2]

**sculpture of a man**
[Praha 1, Josefov, Maiselova 15]

**commemorative plaque of Franz Kafka**
[Praha 1, Staré Město, U radnice 5]

early-Gothic **Staronová Synagogue** dated around the year 1280 as seen from the west, with a brick gable from the 14th century and an outbuilding from the year 1732
*[Praha 1, Josefov, Červená 2]*

**Jewish Town Hall**, at present the seat of Jewish Religious Community, with a small tower and a clock which has Hebrew numerals
*[Praha 1, Josefov, Maiselova 18]*

at the entrance to the Old Jewish Cemetery, there is a pseudo-Romanesque small castle, a building built in the year 1906 which is the **Ceremonial Hall of Funeral Brotherhood** today

*[Praha 1, Josefov, U starého hřbitova 3a]*

the gravestones of the **Old Jewish Cemetery**, one of the most memorable Jewish burial sites in the world. This remarkability of the old Prague came into being through gradual extension of the cemetery founded sometime in the 1st half of the 15th century as a substitution for the original cemetery located outside the city in the place where there is Vladislavova Street at present. It covers an irregularly shaped area and on this area, there are around 20 000 gravestones from the years 1439 to 1787 when burials stopped taking place here

*[Praha 1, Josefov, entrance from the street U starého hřbitova or from Pinkas' Synagogue]*

the majority of the most interesting and artistically most precious gravestones in the **Old Jewish Cemetery** come from the 17th century. On the gravestones, there are very often symbols hewn out indicating to which family the buried person belonged, for example hands - Kohen family, pot - Kohejn family, lion - Levi family, etc., or indicating a trade, for example scissors - tailor, mortar - pharmacist, tweezers - doctor, etc.

*[Praha 1, Josefov, Starý židovský hřbitov]*

below - **gravestone of Hendl Baševi** (†1628), above - **gravestone of rabbi Jehuda Löw Ben Bezalel** (†1609)
*[Praha 1, Josefov, Starý židovský hřbitov]*

jewish kosher **restaurant Šalom** (Shalom)
*[Praha 1, Josefov, Maiselova 18]*

continuous rows of eclectic and Art Nouveau representational apartment houses on **Pařížská boulevard** intersecting the former Jewish ghetto, presently municipal part Josefov, with a panorama of Prague
*[Praha 1, Josefov, view from Orchards of Letná]*

# THE OLD TOWN

The Old Town (Staré Město) whose creation was consummated after the year 1230 by building fortifications around the town area where for two to three centuries, there have been settlements of merchants of Romance origin, of Germans and Jews, surrounding the main Prague market. The consummation of these efforts was a legal unification at he end of the 13th century. Major Town, as it was called at that time, was one of the biggest towns in Europe in respect to its size and economic advancement. After New Town which literally encircled Old Town was founded, a gradual decrease in the Old Town's economic as well as political superiority over the other Prague towns started. However, this decrease was so slow and the tradition was so firm that even in the year 1784 when the Prague was united Old Town Hall became the seat of the all-Prague administration. Up until now, Old Town is regarded as the natural centre of Prague and Old Town Square is regarded as the centre of the city.

However, what was limiting in the old times, that is, the impossibility for the people living in Old Town to expand constructionally, appears from the present architectural point of view as a gift of incalculable value, which is confirmed by such historical monuments as Old Town Astronomical Clock (Staroměstský orloj), Church of Virgin Mary before Týn (kostel P. Marie před Týnem), Powder Gate (Prašná brána), Bethlehem Chapel (Betlémská kaple), but above all, by the uniquely preserved mediaeval built-up area of the whole Old Town.

**house At Golden Crown**
*[Praha 1, Staré Město, Malé náměstí 15]*

**Golz-Kinský Palace**
*[Praha 1, Staré Město, Staroměstské náměstí 11,12]*

**house At Stone Virgin Mary**
*[Praha 1, Staré Město, Staroměstské náměstí 16]*

**sign of Old Town**
*[Praha 1, Staré Město, Staroměstské náměstí 6]*

**new-Baroque facade of the house At Crown**
*[Praha 1, Staré Město, Malé náměstí 13]*

**detail of Old Town Astronomical Clock**
*[Praha 1, Staré Město, Staroměstské náměstí 3]*

globular dome of **St. Francis Seraphine's Church** and **Old Town Bridge Tower**, two of the dominants of the end of the east part of Charles Bridge
[Praha 1, Staré Město, Křižovnické náměstí resp. Karlův most]

Prague Castle as seen from the stairs to **Rudolphinum** built in the years 1876-84 at the expense of Czech Savings Bank
*[Praha 1, Staré Město, náměstí Jana Palacha 1]*

the new-Renaissance building of **Rudolphinum**, which was intended to function as a picture gallery, museum and conservatory, is presently the seat of Czech Philharmonic Orchestra, apart from other things
*[Praha 1, Staré Město, náměstí Jana Palacha 1]*

early-Gothic nave of the St. Salvador's Church situated on the premises of **Anežka's Monastery**. There is also a permanent exhibit of pictures of the National Gallery located in the monastery
*[Praha 1, Staré Město, Anežská 12]*

**embankment Na Františku** in front of which Vltava is crossed by a precision Art Nouveau historical construction, the Bridge of Svatopluk Čech, as seen in nighttime
*[Praha 1, Staré Město, nábřeží Na Františku]*

this is how the Prague Castle can be viewed from **Hlávka's bridge**. The illuminated dome in front belongs to the building that is now the Ministry of Industry and Trade of the Czech Republic

*[Praha 1, Staré Město, Hlávkův most]*

**Powder Tower** and **Municipal House** in the style of Art Nouveau built in the years 1905 - 1911 where, apart from other things, the independence of Czechoslovak Republic was declared on the 28th of Oct. 1918

*[Praha 1, Staré Město, náměstí Republiky 5]*

a theater originally called Nostic' theatre, later on **Theatre of Estates** where the world premiere of the opera Don Giovanni by W. A. Mozart took place in the year 1787
*[Praha 1, Staré Město, Železná 11]*

interior of **St. James' Church** which is in Baroque style today, formerly a monastery of Minorites which was founded by Václav I. in the year 1232 as a Gothic church, which is revealed by the design of the nave

*[Praha 1, Staré Město, Malá Štupartská 6]*

interior of **St. Nicholas' Church** with a crown chandelier, a gift from the Russian Orthodox Church, made of crystal glass in glassworks in Harrachov at the end of the 19th century

*[Praha 1, Staré Město, Staroměstské náměstí - kostel sv. Mikuláše]*

the same **St. Nicholas' Church** and its noble Baroque lines by K. I. Dienzenhofer, built at the expense of Benedictine abbot Anselm Vlach
*[Praha 1, Staré Město, Staroměstské náměstí]*

panoramatic view of the east part of Old Town Square bathing in summer sunlight where
**Church of Virgin Mary before Týn** towers above the whole Old Town. This church,
founded in the middle of the 14th century, became the centre of Prague Chalice Adherents
after the Hussite unrests and this was why it was actually the only church that was given
substantial constructional care at that time. After futile efforts to legalize the Czech Utrakvism,
the importance of the church gradually declined. The interior of the church will capture
the visitor's interest mainly with the abundance of early-Baroque altars and, to mention
a curiosity, there is a grave plaque from the year 1601, the grave plaque of the astronomer
who worked in the court of Rudolph II., the Danish emigrant Tycho de Brahe who was buried here
[Praha 1, Staré Město, Staroměstské náměstí]

above - the **Church of Virgin Mary Before Týn** under which line up the Golz-Kinský Palace and the houses At the Stone Bell, At the Stone Lamb, At the **Golden Unicorn**. Below - a corner house At Unicorn

*[Praha 1, Staré Město, Staroměstské náměstí 11-12, 13, 14, 15, resp. 20]*

below - **St. Nicholas' Church** as seen from a roof of a house in Platnéřská Street. Above - the church of V. Mary Before Týn viewed from Ungelt, right with the Renais. arcade loggia of the **Granovský's house**
*[Praha 1, Staré Město, Staroměstské náměstí resp. Týn 1]*

on the left, there is a tower and the remainder of **Old Town Hall** which, until destroyed by fire in May 1945, formed the whole west side of the square

*[Praha 1, Staré Město, Staroměstské náměstí 3]*

**Old Town Astronomical Clock** which was perfected at the end of the 15th century by Master Hanuš called Rose and which has been up until now frequently renovated
[Praha 1, Staré Město, Staroměstské náměstí 3]

**Bethlehem Chapel** was founded by two Prague patricians, merchant Kříž and Hanuš from Mühlheim for Czech sermons. It is the place where Jan Hus preached
*[Praha 1, Staré Město, Betlémské náměstí 5]*

one of the three rooms of the Romanesque basement of a house pertaining to the former **yard of Lords from Kunštát**
*[Praha 1, Staré Město, Řetězová 3]*

Baroque hall of a former Jesuit library in **Clementinum** which forms the second greatest group of buildings in Prague with castle being the greatest. There are over five million volumes in the library
*[Praha 1, Staré Město, Křižovnické náměstí 4]*

view of Prague Castle, Charles Bridge and the **block of houses of Novotný' Footbridge** with the former mills and a tower of waterworks for Old Town
*[Praha 1, Staré Město, view from Smetana's Embankment]*

# THE NEW TOWN

The New Town (Nové Město) was founded by the emperor Charles IV. in the year 1348. It was the most extensive urbanistic act in Prague and a unique one in the world. In this act, he merged all local settlements from the period of Romanesque style spreading from Těšnov to Vyšehrad and laid the fundamentals of the regulation of the new development which serve up until now without any change. Charles' Square (Karlovo náměstí) was determined to be the main public area whose western side was adjacent to the ancient road leading from Vyšehrad to Prague Castle. Until the time of the Hussite Wars, a religious pilgrimage of European importance which was called "The Showing of Sacraments, Imperial Coronation Jewels and Sacred Remains" took place here every year. This is why the square was planned to cover such an extensive area. However, in the course of time, the area around Můstek which is presently the lower part of Wenceslas Square (Václavské náměstí), the largest and most important Prague's boulevard with important commercial, social and political aspects, gained the economic dominance.

The motives for founding New Town were certainly commercial as well as political. However, it seems that in the first centuries this project had been weak in respect to economy and the cause of this may be for example the Hussite unrests which, apart from other things, had originated in New Town. However, today New Town is a very cultivated area and fully develops the penetrating ideas of its founders.

**sculpture in front of the building of Com.Bank**
[Praha 1, Nové Město, Spálená 51]

**remarkable house of Hlahol society in the Art Nouveau style**
[Praha 1, Nové Město, Masarykovo nábřeží 16]

**new-Baroque modification of the front**
[Praha 2, Nové Město, Masarykovo nábřeží 2]

**sculpture of St. Jan Nepomucký**
[Praha 1, Nové Město, Jindřišská ulice]

**monument of František Palacký, detail**
[Praha 2, Nové Město, Palackého náměstí]

**portal of National Theater with the sculptures of Drama and Opera**
[Praha 1, Nové Město, from Masaryk's Embankment]

the chief Czech dramatic stage, **National Theater**, which was built by architect J. Zítek in the style of late Renaissance in the years 1868-1881 and whose construction was financed from nationwide collections
*[Praha 1, Nové Město, Národní třída 2]*

1000+1 view of Prague Castle. In this case, seen from **Štítkovská Waterworks Tower** and constructivist building Mánes which functions as an exhibition hall and a restaurant
*[Praha 1, Nové Město, Masarykovo nábřeží 1]*

**Na Příkopě Street** which is situated in the place where there were ramparts and a trench protecting Old Town in the Middle Ages. This boulevard came into being in the year 1760 by filling up the trench mentioned.

*[Praha 1, Nové Město, view from Můstek - the lower end of Wenceslas Square]*

**hotels Ambassador**, with the famous Alhambra Bar, and **Zlatá husa** which were built or, more precisely, modernized in the year 1912
*[Praha 1, Nové Město, Václavské náměstí 5, 7]*

music parlour of **Kounický Palace** with the pictures representing the Niebelung myth on the walls
*[Praha 1, Nové Město, Panská 7]*

pantheon in the building of the **National Museum**, commemorating the personalities of Czech nation, where for example four wall paintings represent significant events in Czech history
*[Praha 1, Nové Město, Václavské náměstí 68 - Národní muzeum]*

evening illumination of the building of the National Museum which forms the upper end of **Wenceslas Square**, formerly called Horse Market, which is the largest and busiest Prague boulevard
*[Praha 1, Nové Město, Václavské náměstí]*

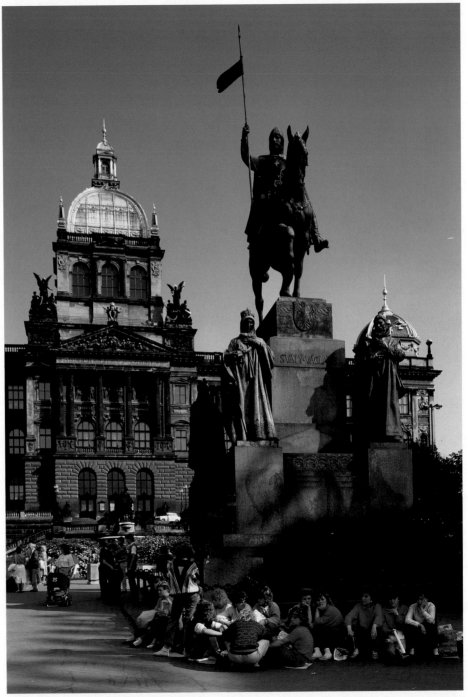

bronze equestrian sculpture by J.V. Myslbek, **monument of St. Wenceslas**, the patron saint of the country, installed here after many problematic public tenders in the year 1913

*[Praha 1, Nové Město, upper part of Wenceslas Square]*

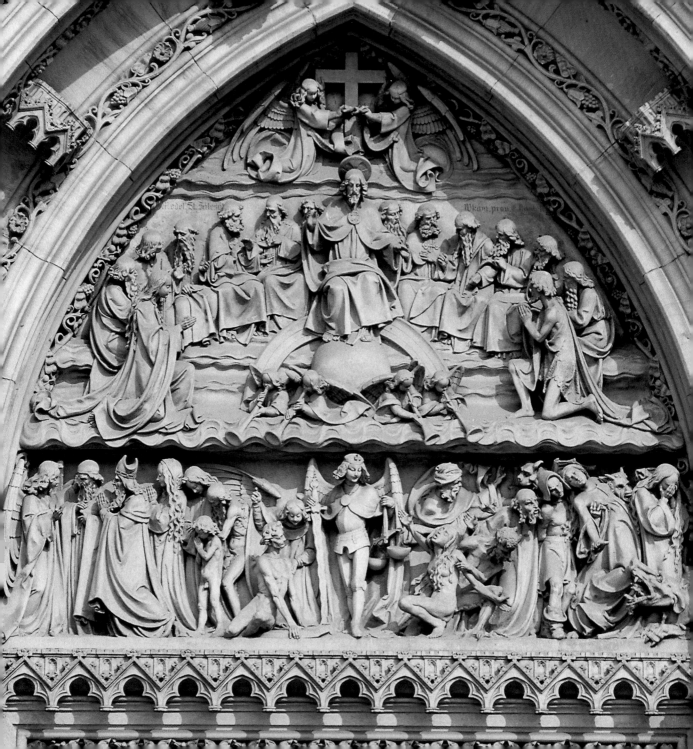

# VYŠEHRAD

Vyšehrad was founded sometime in the 10th century, undoubtedly later than Prague Castle had beem founded and for centuries it also remained in a position subordinate to Prague Castle. This is true perhaps except for the years 1061-1092 when Vyšehrad was the residence of Vratislav II., originally a prince, later the first Czech king, who had the castle reconstructed and made of stone and who set up a church chapter there. Its importance then declined, later on, Charles IV. had Vyšehrad reconstructed and changed into stone fort in connection with the newly built fortification of the whole Prague. However, just as in other places in Bohemia, the life of the castle was negatively influenced by the Hussite period when it was sieged, plundered and partly demolished. In the year 1650, new brick Baroque ramparts were built once again in connection with the fortifying of the whole Prague according to the plans of Italian architects. The castle served as a fort once again until the year 1911 when the fort was abolished. It was annexed to Prague as District VI. in the year 1883.

Vyšehrad is a notable place, if only for its reputation of being the oldest residence of Czech princes, of Libuše and of the first members of Přemysl's dynasty and for the reason that the eminent personalities of the nation are buried there.

**Vltava and Petřín as seen from the ramparts of Vyšehrad**
*[Praha 2, Vyšehrad]*

**portal of the Church of St. Peter and Paul**
*[Praha 2, Vyšehrad]*

**Portal relief with the theme of the Last Judgement**
*[Praha 2, Vyšehrad, kostel sv. Petra a Pavla]*

**Czech lion on a gate**
*[Praha 2, Vyšehrad, kostel sv. Petra a Pavla]*

**Portal pseudo-Gothic sculpture**
*[Praha 2, Vyšehrad, kostel sv. Petra a Pavla]*

**Ctirad and Šárka by J.V. Myslbek**
*[Praha 2, Vyšehrad, orchard of Vyšehrad]*

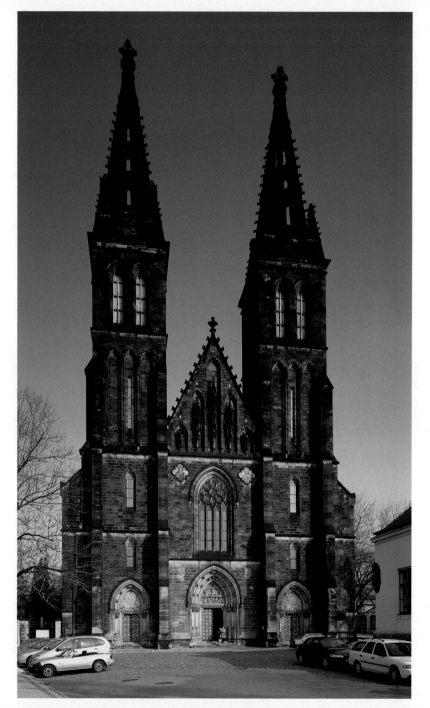

the regothicised, capitular and parish **Church of St. Peter and Paul**, founded as early as in the second half of the 11th century, now with the neo-gothic and Art Nouveau interior
[Praha 2, Vyšehrad, kostel sv. Petra a Pavla]

Wiehl's arcades at the **Vyšehrad cemetery**, a graveyard of outstanding Czech personalities, established in 1869 on the place of an old parish cemetery
[Praha 2, Vyšehrad, Vyšehradský hřbitov]

below - fully preserved Romanesque **St. Martin's rotunda**, the oldest one in Prague, probably from the 11th century. Above - **Leopold's Gate** forming the inner entrance to the fort of Vyšehrad
[Praha 2, Vyšehrad, street V pevnosti]

a view of the **Vyšehrad rock**, enclosed by a five-sided Baroque brick wall, built after 1650 by Italian architects
*[Praha 2, Vyšehrad]*

# OTHERS

Others is a part containing the historical monuments and architectonic treasures of Prague which you can find when sightseeing the other districts of the city. St. Margareth's Monastery (klášter U sv. Markéty), Zbraslav Chateau, St. Ludmila's Church (kostel sv. Ludmily), Chateau Summerhouse Troja, Summerhouse Hvězda, Bertramka, Jesus Heart's Church (kostel Srdce Ježíšova), but also Hanavský Pavilion, Křižík's Fountain, Corinthia Hotel, Congress Centre (Kongresové centrum) and Business Centre are their representatives. However, some of them are very significant representatives such as St. Margareth's Monastery, also called Břevnov Monastery, whose present Baroque appearance came into being in the years 1708 to 1745. Or the Summerhouse Hvězda in whose vicinity the last phase of the significant "Battle on Bílá Hora" took place in the year 1620. The Chateau Summerhouse Troja is an excellent place for an excursion, if only for its vicinity to the Prague Zoo. Zbraslav and its chateau where, long ago, Václav II. liked to stay is no less popular.

The surroundings of the historical Prague are not, of course, as attractive as its centre, however, I believe that seeing the valuable historical monuments mentioned above will satisfy you and will supplement the mosaic which we put together in the preceding seven parts.

**entrance gate of St. Margareth's Monastery**
[Praha 6, Břevnov, Markétská 28]

**grave plaque of hermit Vintíř**
[Praha 6, Břevnov, klášter U sv. Markéty]

**part of the exhibition of Czech plastic art**
[Praha 5, Zbraslav, zámek Zbraslav]

**sculpture by B. Stefan above the portal of the church**
[Praha 3, Vinohrady, kostel Srdce Ježíšova]

**parish Church of Jesus' Heart**
[Praha 3, Vinohrady, náměstí Jiřího z Poděbrad]

**portal of St. Ludmila's Church**
[Praha 2, Vinohrady, náměstí Míru]

Baroque constructions of Benedictine **St. Margareth's Monastery**, the first monastery of men in Bohemia, founded by the second Prague bishop Vojtěch and prince Boleslav II in the year 993
*[Praha 6, Břevnov, Markétská 28]*

**chateau Summerhouse Troja** built in the style of Baroque Classicism with rich ceiling and wall paintings. The summerhouse is open to the public, including the permanent exhibit of the National Gallery
*[Praha 7, Troja, U Trojského zámku 6]*

above - **Summerhouse Hvězda** in Renaissance style with an unusual ground plan in the shape of a star - authored by archduke Ferdinand of Tyrol. Below - **Bertramka**, a place where Mozart used to stay frequently.

[Praha 6, Liboc, game park Hvězda / Praha 5, Smíchov, Mozartova 2]

above - one of the floors of the former assembly hall
of a monastery, presently Royal Hall of **Zbraslav Chateau**,
with an exhibit of Czech plastic art of National Gallery.
Below - **Hanavský Pavilion** with a cast-iron skeleton
which was moved here and re-installed in the year 1898
*[Praha 5, Zbraslav / Praha 7, Letná, orchards of Letná ]*

above - **Křižík's Fountain** on the Prague Exhibition Site, harmonized with a musical accompaniment. Below - the buildings of **Corinthia Tow. Hotel** and **Congress Centrum** on a hill in the district of Pankrác
*[Praha 7, Holešovice, street U Výstaviště / Praha 4, Pankrác, Kongresová 1 resp. 5. května 65]*

ve - a group of supermodern build. Of the **Business Centre** behind Hilton-Atrium Hotel. Below - postmodernist **Dancing house**. It's constr. in 1992-96 was financed by insurance comp. Nationale Nederlanden
*[Praha 8, Karlín, Pobřežní 3 / Praha 2, Nové Město, Rašínovo nábřeží 80]*